CW00550208

Easter People

*Inspirational Poems
for Personal Reflection and Prayer*

R.J. HÉTU

Copyright © 2022 by R.J. Hétu.

Cover photo
Cathedral Basilica of Christ the King
Hamilton, Ontario, Canada
Taken by the author
May 2007

ISBN 978-1-957781-46-4 (softcover)
ISBN 978-1-957781-47-1 (ebook)
Library of Congress Control Number: 2022905014

All rights reserved. No part of this book may be reproduced or transmitted in any form or by any means, electronic or mechanical, including photocopying, recording, or by any information storage and retrieval system without express written permission from the author, except in the case of brief quotations embodied in critical reviews and certain other noncommercial uses permitted by copyright law.

Printed in the United States of America.

Book Vine Press
2516 Highland Dr.
Palatine, IL 60067

To The Greater Glory of God

In Memory of my parents

Jean-Marie Hétu
1927–2002

Thérèse (Courchesne) Hétu
1929–2007

Foreword

BISHOP OF HAMILTON

Father Robert Hétu is a man of faith and he is a poet. Poets use the language to express insights and deeper reflections in creative ways, capturing what is often inexpressible otherwise. Hétu, a French-speaker, has mastered the English language to the degree that his thoughts and insights, presented in a variety of poetic and literary forms, are readily accessible.

These poems are reflections; they are prayers; they are stories – and they all capture the imagination and stir the soul! Read each one slowly – reflectively. You will get to know this Priest and his spirituality. His writing will lift you up and inspire you. Even better, it will draw you to an encounter with the Lord, who is very present throughout the book.

Poetry is a perfect way to express the divine experience of God's presence in our world and in our life. We are an Easter People! This book of gems helps us understand what that means and what a blessing it is in our lives!

Bishop Douglas Crosby, OMI
Bishop of Hamilton

700 King St. West, Hamilton, Ontario, Canada L8P 1C7

Preface

January 1, 2022

Dear Readers,

I never really liked poetry when I was a schoolboy. I thought all that rhyming was too difficult. So, it is hard to believe that this is my second book of poetry to be published. My first book, in 2003, entitled *The Blood Of His Love*, was the result of my preaching and teaching ministry. Back in the early 2000's, I was encouraged by my parishioners to put my poems together in a book and so I compiled 75 poems for that first book.

This present compilation, that I entitled *An Easter People* has taken me much longer to compile and publish. It has been in the works for 'at least dozen years' or so. Life as a Catholic priest can be busy and very hectic. So, I am happy to have finally completed this project.

Currently, my focus is on faith-based poetry for personal reflection and prayer. I have been inspired by my prayer life, spiritual reading, and the good old internet. Many of the ideas of my poems are influenced by others, and of course the Bible, therefore, I try to give credit to those who inspired me. My poetry is an evolving art. Thirty to forty of the current poems are reprints or modifications of poems from my first book.

This compilation of 185 poems covers a multitude of styles and approaches. Like my hockey career, which I began in the seminary at the age of 21, I really never played ice hockey before, I only began writing poetry seriously as a priest in my early forties. Over the years, by God's grace, I have come to the realization that poetry is more than rhyming. Poetry is speaking from the heart.

Some poems were easy to write others not so. The fastest poem I wrote, on a lark, is *A Goalie's Prayer*. It might have taken me five minutes. The poem that took the longest to write is my four-line poem *Four Seasons*. This one took me over three years to finish. I had three seasons covered, but the fourth season took forever.

A special thanks to my former secretary Bonnie Maloney, who first encouraged me to put my poetry in print. (It all started in the parish bulletin.) Thanks also to Dorice Haché, another former secretary, who had a copy of most of my poems, many of which I no longer had. Thanks also to Annette Raby, cook extraordinaire, for her encouragement and proof reading of the current compilation.

Remember to please take time to meditate on each poem and let the Holy Spirit lead you wherever she wills.

Shalom,

Fr. Robert Hétu
Welland, Ontario
curé/Pastor
Of the four French language parishes
in the Niagara Region

Contents

A.B.C.'s Of Faith

(Dedicated to the memory of my mother Thérèse)

Accept God's love

Believe the Good News

Communicate what you hear

Open to the Spirit

Friend of Jesus

Faithful to the Father

Acceptance of others

Intimacy with the poor

Truth leading the way

Hope in eternal life

2019

A Disciple
(Inspired by Josh Hunt)

Always

Disciplined

Intimate friend of Jesus

Sacrificial Giver

Community worshiper

Intimate family member

Passion for others

Lover of God

Evangelistic involvement

2018

A Foretaste Of Heaven

(Inspired by St. Jean-Marie Vianney, Patron Saint of Priests)

Prayer is honey
    that flows into the soul
        and makes all things sweet

Through it we receive
    a foretaste of heaven
        and union with God

Union with God
    is a happiness
        beyond all understanding

To pray and love
    that is where lies
        our treasure and serenity

2011

A Gift

(A traditional cinquain)

The rose
A gift from God
Dressed in exquisite red
Reflecting the Maker's beauty
And love

2005

A Goalie's Prayer

Life can be sticky
In ice hockey
Away from the board
I turn to the Lord

With gloves together
I say a prayer
Down on one knee
I reverently plea

Let them score
No more
For lowly me
Am goalie

When one behaves
Jesus saves

Amen

2019

A New Spring

Relaxing
    on the dew soaked
        summer-like
            green grass

Enjoying
    the rainbow
        of autumn colours
            dancing in the breeze

Listening to
    the whistle
        of roaring waters
            rushing by

Slowly lingering
    in the stale air
        the sad stench
            of lifeless winter

Yet, ultimately rejoicing
    in the sun's
        delicious promises
            of a new spring

2009

A Reflection Of Heaven

From the darkness of night
Arises streaks of golden light
Seabirds chant their morning praise
As the sun overtakes the haze

A rhapsody of white spray
Brings joy and peace our way
For this kaleidoscope of colour
We give God thanks and honour

These awesome gifts are given
As a reflection of heaven
In our longing for perfection
We marvel in sacred creation

Helping us to daily cope
And glory in our heavenly hope
Focusing on our destiny
To share in God's eternity

2011

A Red Rose

(Inspired by Becca)

A most beautiful rose
In glorious red clothes
Says, 'I love you'
And 'you're special' too

Though the thorns may cause pain
Our joy we can regain
By the grace of forgiveness
And so revert to happiness

A red rose tells of beauty
And of God's majesty
A treasure to share
If we take time to care

A red rose can cause a smile
That will last a long while
So let us share this gift
Giving a loved one a lift

A most beautiful rose
In glorious red clothes
Says, 'I love you'
And 'you're special' too

2019

A Sun That Never Sets

Let your grace
    be a sun
        that never sets

As an offering
    we dedicate
        this day

May Your gift
    of light daily
        guide our way

Remain with us
    the whole day
        O Lord

Fashioning us into
    salt for the earth
        and light for our world

May the love
    of the Holy Spirit
        direct our hearts

To always act
    according to
        Your sacred will

Do not let us
    offer anything
        that is evil

Lord make us
    instruments of
        Your lasting peace

Let your grace
    be a sun
        that never sets

2019

A Virtuous Garden

Plant the seeds of faith
Forever cultivate hope
And you'll harvest love

2008

All Are Welcome

Yes all are welcome
So come as you are
From near or afar
Just be sure to come

We are not here to judge
Come before it's too late
Your future is great
Now take this little nudge

No need to worry or fuss
We want to share God's love
A gift from heaven above
So come and pray with us

Church is open to all
Saints and sinners
Yes even faith beginners
Just answer the call

So be sure to come
To church this Sunday
Join us without delay
Remember all are welcome
2003

All Creatures Praise The Lord

(Inspired by and adapted from Daniel 3)

All creatures, praise the Lord
Angels in heaven, praise the Lord
Sun and moon, praise the Lord
Stars above, praise the Lord

Morning dew, praise the Lord
The four winds, praise the Lord
Frost and chill, praise the Lord
Ice and snow, praise the Lord

Fire and heat, praise the Lord
Lightning and thunder, praise the Lord
Clouds and rain, praise the Lord
All four seasons, praise the Lord

Light and darkness, praise the Lord
Mountains and hills, praise the Lord
Valleys and plains, praise the Lord
Vegetation of the earth, praise the Lord

Rivers and springs, praise the Lord
Seas and oceans, praise the Lord
All water creatures, praise the Lord
Birds of the air, praise the Lord

All wild beasts, praise the Lord
Tame animals, too, praise the Lord
People of the earth, praise the Lord
All humble of heart, praise the Lord

Servants of God, praise the Lord
Spirits and souls, praise the Lord
Saints in heaven, praise the Lord
Yes, all creatures of God, praise the Lord

2017

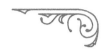

All I Am I Offer

All that I am I offer now to You
That I may be transformed to serve You true
Be my faithful guide and beacon of light
Allowing me to spend eternity in Your sight

Jesus this is why You came down to earth
To lead me, reminding me of my worth
Dying on the cross and not counting the cost
You won salvation for me so I would not be lost

Please remind me daily my Saving Lord
To live with others in one accord
Promoting peace and justice for us all
Forever answering Your heavenly call

2019

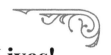

Alleluia! Alleluia! Jesus Lives!

Alleluia! Alleluia! Jesus lives!
My sins God forgives
No questions asked
I am completely unmasked

I am what I am
You chose to be my Sacrificial Lamb
To overcome my mortal combat
And, I thank You Lord for that

I cherish all Your blessings
Help me to remember Your teachings
Being aware of Your gift of the Tree
Help me live as You call me to be

Despite the hardships of The Way
You will never lead me astray
Yes, new life Jesus gives
Alleluia! Alleluia! Jesus lives!

2007

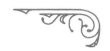

Always Near

(Inspired by Psalm 18)

Lord how I love You
Without You what can I do
When in trouble I call, You hear
For I know You are always near

You are my defender
And my great protector
To You Lord I yield
Because You are my shield

From my enemies' plots and harm
You save me by Your mighty arm
Yes for all my days
Lord I give you praise

2004

An Awesome Reflection

The
Red rose
A gift from
God up above
Sign of God's true love
Dressed in exquisite clothes
Simplistic beautifulness
Thank You gracious Creator God
Truly this glorious red rose is
An awesome reflection of the Maker

2019

An Easter People

For you and me
Jesus came to earth
From sin to set us free
And give us new birth

Despite His pain and strife
Out of love for us all
Jesus gave up His life
Answering the Father's call

After three days in the tomb
He rose on that third day
Overcoming our despair and gloom
Showing us the way

From the highest steeple
Let us boldly proclaim
We are an Easter People
And be proud of our name

2010

An Ode To John The Baptist

A drunken oath of a king
    With a shallow sense of honour
        A seductive sexy dance
A vengeful heart of a queen
    Combined to bring about
        The martyrdom of this great prophet

His vocation was one of selfless giving
    He claimed no self-power or authority
        This man never allowed himself false honour
His calling was one of preparation
    Sharing a message of eternal hope
        Yet living most simply and humbly

As a 'voice crying in the wilderness'
    He did not hesitate to accuse the guilty
        Nor compromise in speaking the truth
'I baptized with water for repentance
    But the one coming after me is greater
        I am unworthy to untie his sandals'

A drunken oath of a king
    With a shallow sense of honour
        A seductive sexy dance
A vengeful heart of a queen
    Combined to bring about
        The martyrdom of this great prophet

Boldly before two of his disciples he witnessed
'Behold the Lamb of God!'
    Then the two disciples turned and followed Jesus
It was John who pointed the way to Christ
    His heart was centred on God alone
        Through the guidance of the Holy Spirit

John's life and death were given in selfless love
    To prepare the people for the promised Messiah
        Glorify God by assisting the salvation of others
Jesus, himself said of his faithful cousin
    'No one born of woman is greater than he'
        A great model and witness for all times

A drunken oath of a king
    With a shallow sense of honour
        A seductive sexy dance
A vengeful heart of a queen
    Combined to bring about
        The martyrdom of this great prophet

2011

At Easter

The beauty and promise
    of the Resurrection
Are reflected now in nature
    as spring awakens in glory

Each blade of grass and
    bud that blooms
Reaches up to God in
    wondrous praise

At Easter as in spring
    miraculous things happen
When we simply open
    ourselves to God

May the sacrifice of Jesus
    on the Cross
With the glorious miracle
    of the empty tomb

Deepen within us faith,
hope and love
So we can share in the new life
of the Risen Jesus

May the blessings of the Lord
be for ever upon us
As we celebrate the new dawn
Easter brings the world

Yes, Jesus has died, Jesus is Risen
Jesus will come again
Let us for ever sing
Alleluia! Alleluia! Alleluia!

2016

At My Side

Lord, You are my saving shelter
With You I shall never falter
Blanket me with Your gift of love
A heavenly mantle from above

Contemplating Your sacred chimes
Lord, You keep me safe at all times
From my enemies I need not hide
For You are always at my side

2019

Be Still And Know

Be still and know that I am God
Like a Shepherd I lead my sheep
I watch over you with my rod
From all danger my sheep I keep

Come to me if you are burdened
Take my yoke upon your shoulder
Your heavy load I have lightened
Your many prayers I answer

I will always seek and find you
No matter how far you wander
Your rebel heart I will subdue
For I am a forgiving Father

Your love and sorrow will suffice
My Son already paid the price

2003

Blessed Are You Lord

(Inspired by 1 Chronicles 29)

O God eternal
Grandeur and power are yours
Blessed are You Lord

For all in heaven
And on earth glorify You
Blessed are You Lord

Riches and honour
Come from You and You alone
Blessed are You Lord

We give You thanks Lord
Your hands are power and might
Blessed are You Lord

Majesty is Yours
We praise Your glorious name
Blessed are You Lord

2017

Blessed Seasons
(Two traditional cinquains)

Noël

Christmas
Let us rejoice
For our Saviour was born
To set us free from all our sins
Amen

Paschal

Easter
Season of joy
For our Lord Jesus died
And is risen to set us free
Amen

2005

Blessings Of Life

(Based on – Rowyn's Tree of Life – Author Unknown)

I will honour the blessings of life
The blessings of life
That are found in the trees
In the greens of the leaves
In the flight of the birds
In the smell of the fertile soil

I will honour the blessings of life
The blessings of life
That glow in fire
That fall in the rain
That blow in the wind
That rest in the earth

I will honour the blessings of life
In the eyes of God
I will remember who I am
And what I keep holy
I will always honour
The blessings of life

2019

Carpe Diem

Listen to the whisper of the dawn
The rising sun and morning calm,
Seize this day for it is rife
It is the very essence of life

In its short and brief interlude
All truths and realities are accrued
Bliss of growth and splendour of beauty
Reward of action and glory to be

For yesterday is but an old dream
So, let today reign supreme
For tomorrow is only a glim vision
Yet, no future if today is not liven

A today fully lived and experienced makes
All yesterdays happy keepsakes
And all tomorrows promises to bloom
Such is the cry of the dawn. Carpe diem!

2003

Christmas

Came down from

Heaven

Royal King

Incarnate

Son of God

The long awaited

Messiah

And

Saviour—Jesus Christ

2002

Come Into My Light

Come into My light
Do not remain in the dark
Come and share My life

Come into My light
To clearly see the right path
The road to follow

Come into My light
Let me show you once again
My hopes, plans and dreams

Come into My light
Surrender all your worries
As you find My way

Come into My light
Experience for yourself
The peace of My love

Come into My light
As you are—worthy or not
Share in My mercy

Come into My light
With love I endured the Cross
To save you from sin

Come into My light
From the grave I am Risen
Bringing you new life

Come into My light
To heaven I ascended
Now with Our Father

Come into My light
That I may pour over you
My grace upon grace

Come into My light
Let My love for ever warm
Your longing still heart

Come into My light
Do not remain in the dark
Come and share My life

2019

Come To Me

Come to Me
Come and see

> If you are weary
> Or even teary
> Your burden heavy
> Come I levy
> I am gentle
> Non-judgemental

Humble in heart
Peace I impart

> My yoke is easy
> My nature breezy
> My burden light
> Making all right
> My one only goal
> Rest for your soul

Come and see
Come to Me

2002

Colours Of Creation

From chaos to light
Creation is awoken
Morning sun ablaze

Under azure skies
Valleys of teeming new life
A beautiful sight

From the budding branch
The crimson cardinal chants
The praises of spring

A kaleidoscope
Of bright colourful flowers
A summer delight

As the sunlight fades
Contemplating creation
I give God glory

2010

Dear Guardian Angel

(An adapted prayer)

Angel of God, my Guardian dear
To whom God's love commits me here
Be ever at my side this day
To light, guide and guard my way

Amen

2016

Dear Jesus

Dear Jesus, be a stranger
In my life no longer
O, come into my heart
Please help me to restart

Dear Jesus, You have been there
Faithfully beyond compare
Foolishly, I have wandered
Without You I'm not anchored

Dear Jesus, I am blinded
I'm alone and defeated
All I see is the darkness
My life is totally aimless

Dear Jesus, help me find You
With You I can start anew
Now, I know Your ways are true
Grant me Your grace and virtue

Dear Jesus, please forgive me
Help me follow You boldly
To impart Your Holy Name
Everywhere and without shame

Dear Jesus, be a stranger
In my life no longer
O, come into my heart
Please help me to restart

2005

Exalt And Rejoice

(Inspired by Psalm 31)

Indeed You're my Rock
A strong Fortress to save me
A Rock of refuge

You are my Fortress
Yes, for Your name's sake lead me
Be my guiding Light

You have redeemed me
I commit my lowly heart
Into Your safe hands

O saving Shelter
Let Your face shine steadfast love
Upon your servant

O Lord, faithful God
I will exalt and rejoice
Trusting You always

2006

Faith, Hope And Love
(A humble prayer—remembering 9-11)

Lord make me an instrument of peace
Ease my worries and my burdens release
With faith I believe in Your power dear God
You protect me with Your Shepherd's rod

Hope, my optimism for now and tomorrow
For with You, I can overcome any sorrow
With love, the greatest of all Your gifts
My heart, my mind and soul, it lifts

Please endow me with faith, hope and love
Your powerful gifts from heaven above
Into Your loving hands I commend my spirit
Please bless us all beyond our merit

Amen

2002

For All Eternity

(A prayer inspired by Saint John Henry Newman)

My God, how far am I from acting according to what I know so well
I confess it, my heart goes after too many dark shadows
Rouse me from complacency and make me desire only You
Help me to open my whole heart to Your bountiful and
   redemptive graces
Teach me to love meditation, sacred scripture, spiritual reading
   and prayer
Teach me Your love, which shall engage my mind and soul
   for all eternity

Amen

2017

Forgive And Forget

To love is to commit
Be prepared not to quit
Forgive and forget
Or retain and regret

To fail is natural
To let go supernatural
Forgive and forget
Or retain and regret

In good times and bad
Even if you are mad
Forgive and forget
Or retain and regret

Let go of the hurt
To happiness revert
Forgive and forget
Or retain and regret

Love is forever
Never say never
Forgive and forget
Or retain and regret

2002

Forgiveness

We must learn to forgive
And to truly forget
So, let us really live
And love with no regret

With forgiveness is pain
It cost Jesus His life
Considering what we gain
For us, it's worth the strife

True love takes time to give
The gift of forgiveness
It allows us to live
Free of all bitterness

Forgiveness is a must
Like Jesus let us trust

2003

Four Seasons

The wild winds and woolly
   Winter wonder
Surrender to the slow and silent
   serendipity of Spring
So too, the sizzling and scorching
   sun of Summer
Awakens the awesome aurora
   of Autumn a blazing

2006

From Ashes To New Life

*(Dedicated to the parishioners of St. Joseph
Patron of Canada Parish, Acton, Ontario)*

Branches intertwined
Into a crown of sharp thorns
You wore it for me

Eerie darkened clouds
Haunting lifeless blackened sky
Your death remembered

You are my fortress
My rock-solid foundation
Guide and direct me

Prune away all things
That make me coarse and bitter
Leaving your sweet love

Lord Jesus draw me
From the dark ashes of death
To light and new life

Your most Holy Cross
And miraculous rising
Frees us from our sins

Dear Jesus lead me
From death to resurrection
And Easter glory

2018

From Chaos To Light

Creation was awoken
And God had spoken
From total confusion
God did an act of fusion

From chaos to light
Came day and night
Dawn's early light
Our morning delight

Night, moon and stars
God lovingly made ours
They are gifts of love
From heaven up above

2002

From Lent To Easter

(Dedicated to the parishioners of St. Patrick's Parish,
Burlington, Ontario)

The season of Lent
Is time to repent
To prepare the way
For that Special Day

Jesus took up His cross
Which seemed like a loss
And despite His personal pain
We have everything to gain

So, let us use these forty days
For fasting, almsgiving and praise
May His cross circumvent
Our eternal descent

Let us use His hurt
To help us convert
May we always be aware
Of His unconditional loving care

May this self-sacrificing event
Reveal our heart's true intent
To change our direction
And eternally celebrate His Resurrection

2002

Generous Spirit

(Inspired by Rose Marie Morris)

As we left the restaurant the other day
We realized that things are not always as they seem
A homeless man asked us to help him if we may
Changeless I gave him five dollars to my friend's dismay
But left the stranger with a smile and eyes agleam

As I walked to the parking lot booth he followed me
Offering some of his change to pay for the parking
With a great big 'thank you' I declined you see
The restaurant had stamped my card already
So there's no need for us to do a second paying

Later my friend marvelled at the man's generous spirit
Here he was truly in need but still wanted to share
Perhaps one day together we will taste the heavenly banquet
The real prize for us to treasure way beyond our merit
I saw Jesus in the poor man's face and knew he would care

2004

Glory To God

Glory to God on high
We praise Thee, God most nigh
Peace on earth and good will to all
As we heed Thy call

We glorify Thee
We give thanks to Thee
For Thy great glory
Heavenly Father most worthy

Lord Jesus Christ the Son
Lamb of God, only begotten One
Have mercy, have mercy on us
And take our sins away from us

Sitting at the right hand of the Father
Receive our humble prayer
For Thou Lord Jesus alone are holy
And we give Thee praise and glory

Jesus, bless us beyond our merit
With the gift of Thy Holy Spirit
As we bow before Thy heavenly altar
In glory to God our Father

2003

Glory To God For Ever

(Inspired by and adapted from F. Pratt Green)

Jesus is the Way, He and no other
Born in our darkness, He became our Brother
If we see Him, we see God the Father
Glory to God for ever

Jesus is the Truth, He and no other
With Him we will never falter
He unites us to God the Father
Glory to God for ever

Jesus is the Life, He and no other
Sold for silver and murdered, our Brother
Rising He saves us and reigns with God the Father
Glory to God for ever

Glory to the Trinity, God and none other
Glory to God, for the gift of Jesus our Brother
Glory to God, Spirit, Son and Father
Glory to God for ever

2005

Glory to God Our Father

Glory to God our Father
Your glory is overflowing
You made heaven and earth
You sent into the world
Your only Son Jesus Christ
Who gives us eternal life

By the gifts of the Holy Spirit
We are all united together
To give praise and sing
Tribute to the Holy Trinity
Hear our prayers of worship
Glory to You—God our Father

2019

God Is Steadfast

(Inspired by Psalm 66)

Bless God, O peoples
The sound of God's praise be heard
May our feet not slip

Everyone come; hear
As I tell what God has done
For me on this day

Blessed be the Lord
My prayer was accepted
Filled with God's great love

God's love is faithful
The Lord has kept us alive
God reigns for ever

Yes, let all the earth
Cry out to our God with joy
For God is steadfast

2019

God's Precious Lamb

Jesus is my Shepherd
I am God's precious lamb
Part of God's chosen herd
Yes that is who I am

God safely leads me home
Caring for me always
Giving me sacred shalom
I am true to God's ways

Guided by God's true light
I stay on the right path
Forever day and night
Protected from God's wrath

I am God's precious lamb
Yes that is who I am

2019

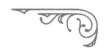

Hail Mother Mary

Hail Mother Mary
You are full of grace
You are my friend
I love you without end

You are the Chosen One
Be with me on my life journey
Listen to my prayers and fears
May they find a place in your heart

Dear Mary Mother of God
Help me to get to heaven
I thank and praise you Blessed Lady
Giving glory to God—Trinity most blest

2019

He Had A Crown

He had a crown
And royal gown
Of crimson red
To His throne was led

> Not a golden crown
> Or regal gown
> But a crown of thorns
> And rags He adorns

Atmosphere dense
Scene very tense
Situation stemmed
He was condemned

> Punishment a cross
> Now complete chaos
> There was screaming
> And some weeping

He had a crown
And royal gown
Of crimson red
To His throne was led

> Nailed to a tree
> Painful agony
> To His Father cried
> Out of love He died

Placed in a tomb
World full of gloom
Time of sadness
Days of darkness

>   Three days later
>   He is our Saviour
>   Rising from the dead
>   To heaven we are led

He had a crown
And royal gown
Of crimson red
To His throne was led

>   Despite His strife
>   We have new life
>   His wooden throne
>   Is our new birthstone

Always loving
Christ is now King
Our strong anchor
That we honour

Grace You impart
Giving us a new heart
To love and serve You
And forever be true

He had a crown
And royal gown
Of crimson red
To His throne was led

2005

Heartfelt Prayer

A little prayer has great power
It surely can be made at any hour
If we wish to attain prayer's goal
We must put in heart and soul

My prayer makes sweet my sour heart
And merry my lonely sad heart
It fills my cold heart with God's warm light
And my blind heart with God's heavenly light

Two special lovers are brought together
Through our timely and heartfelt prayer
God from heaven and our yearning soul
United with the Lord we become whole

Lord, make my sometimes foolish heart wise
Able to accept Your sacred heavenly prize
My salvation that You for me have won
Thank You Jesus; may Your will always be done

Amen

2003

Heavenly Angels

(Inspired by St. Gregory the Great, Pope)

Jesus, our Saviour, King of Angels
Mary, our Mother, Queen of Angels
May all heavenly Angels forever attend us
Guiding and shielding us from every evil

St. Michael, Prince of Angels
Come down amongst the people
Archangel Michael—*who is like God*
Protect us, defend us and bring us peace

St. Gabriel, heavenly messenger
Come down from heaven
Archangel Gabriel—*strength of God*
Enlighten our hearts and minds

St. Raphael, guide our daily actions
From our inner blindness of sin
Archangel Raphael—*remedy of God*
Heal our bodies and souls

Guardian Angels protect us
Angels of Good surround us
Angels of Love comfort us
Angels of the Lord bless us

2018

Heavenly Gardener

Out of chaos and nothingness
God the heavenly Gardener
Sent the bright gift of Jesus the Son
And poured down the Holy Spirit
As a spring of living-water

The Father plants the virtues
Seeds of faith, hope and love
Through the fertile soil of prayer
These seeds are nourished and grow
And weaken the weeds of sin

Fertilized by the grace of the Word
And the special food of the Eucharist
Our plants bloom and flourish
Producing fruit that will last
The fruit of the Holy Spirit

The life-source of a virtuous garden
Is God the heavenly Gardener
Enlightened by Jesus the Son
And watered by the Holy Spirit
United together as One

2014

Heavenly Sent

(Inspired by a tweet on Twitter)

Let us be nourished
By the bright rays of God's Son
Planted in our hearts

All of the flowers
Of every tomorrow
Are in today's seeds

Heavenly sent gift
Is the beauty of the heart
Deep within our soul

2019

Heavenly Whispers

(Based on a circulating e-mail)

One night a man prayed,
"God, please speak to me"
A scarlet cardinal sang
But, the man did not hear

> The next day, the man said
> "God, speak to me"
> A roaring thunder rolled
> Across the azure sky
> But, the man did not listen

Later that evening,
The man looked around and cried
"God please let me see you"
A star shone brightly
But, the man did not see

> Still the man shouted
> "God show me a miracle"
> A child was born
> But, the man did not notice

So, the man yelled out in despair,
"Touch me God
I need to know you're here"
Where upon, God reached down
And touched him
But, the man brushed off the butterfly
And sadly walked away

2005

Hesitant Whispers

(Inspired by reading Word Among Us)

Lord, hear the hesitant
    whispers of my heart
Remove from me my rags
    of darkness and shame

Bathe me in your rivers
    of grace and love
To once again drink deeply
    from Your springs of mercy

Help me put on Your radiant
    mantle of joy
And free my tongue
    to sing Your praises

2010

I Am What I Am

Faithful to my many colours
The rainbow leads me
I might not conform to the mold
Yet, I am what I am

In the palm of your hands
You love me as you have created me
A unique work of art
An 'unparalleled' creation

You call me to experience
Your love and your forgiveness
To share your Good News
Making you known throughout the world

I thank you, Lord
For having loved me to your death
I am aware that death
Has no more power over you nor me

I beseech you Lord, help me
To share your new life
And your promise of heaven
With everyone that I meet

May the gift of the Eucharist
Be our nourishment for the journey
Lord, I thank you
That I am what I am

2019

I Miss You

(In memory of Fr. Richard Hurdle 1957–2012)

I miss you

It was only yesterday that we said hello
I thought it would be forever
Yet, the Lord had other plans
You were called home to be with him

You were the one with whom I shared my heart
Today without you I'm a little scared
As my confidant you were my anchor
My dear friend I miss you

Still I am a person of great faith
I trust God's love and eternal plan
I do not say 'goodbye' but 'adieu'
We will see each other again in heaven

I really miss you

2019

I Need You, Jesus

I really truly need You
I need Your constant love
My days and life without You
Are sad and completely blue
You're my answer from above

I have finally come to realize
That You truly care for me
I am special in Your eyes
You care for me as a prize
With You I am absolutely free

You help me accept my weaknesses
And make my conversion last
Your virtues to guide me are endless
Your support and comfort gratis
So, I can leave the past in the past

My future spiritual growth is in You
And Your constant help from above
By grace, I will stick to You like glue
And my blessings will forever accrue
Thank You, Lord Jesus for Your love

2003

I Praise You Jesus

O Jesus Christ the Son
Lord, for you I long
My victory You have won
With You I'm truly strong

With joy I sing Your praise
All laud and honour are due
My arms in prayer I raise
All glory and power to You

Lord lead me to Your peace
As I glorify You each day
With words that never cease
May I always continue to pray

Yes, I worship You in song
To You my spirit I commend
With You alone I belong
Amen! Alleluia! Amen!

2002

I Trust In The Lord

(Based on Psalm 52)

So why do you boast
You champion of evil
Master of deceit

You love destruction
And evil more than goodness
Lies more than the truth

Uprooting evil
From the land of the living
God will destroy you

God will remove you
God will snatch you from your tent
To punish your crimes

I for evermore
In the presence of God's friends
Proclaim God's name good

In the house of God
Like a growing olive tree
I trust in the Lord

2011

I Trust In You Lord

(Inspired by Psalm 40)

I trust in You Lord
You rescued me from the pit
You answered my pleas

From the miry clay
You set my feet upon rock
Made my footsteps firm

I will praise You Lord
With a new song You gave me
And put on my lips

I trust in You Lord
Many forever fear You
Happy those who trust

To all the peoples
Your justice I have proclaimed
In You I delight

With many blessings
You still work wonders for me
You have no equal

I trust in You Lord
Your merciful love and truth
Will always guard me.

My lips are not sealed
I declare your faithful help
It's never hidden

Lord, come to my aid.
Let there be gladness and joy
For You Lord are great

2019

I Will Always Love You

(Inspired by a poem of an unknown author)

Do not cry for me my friend
We know this is not really the end
Do not be sad and blue
I will always love you

Keep your eyes focused on God above
Remembering the Father's continuous love
Honouring the Holy Spirit and Jesus the Son
And the gift of salvation that for us Jesus won

I am once again whole and at peace
Here my joy will never cease
My loving heart is still with you
Preparing a special place for you

God will call you too, one day
To this heavenly dwelling up and away
And we will once again be together
Praising God side by side and for ever

2017

I Would Like...

(Inspired by Estaban Sanchez)

I would like…
To be the words of a melody
A joyful song full of harmony
Perhaps a bold strong wind
Or soft subtle breeze
To calm your many fears
And all your great worries

I would like…
To be a fire and burn your chains
Cleanse you with life-giving water
And ease your pains
My Special Friend I want you to meet
If you befriend Him
He'll make your life aglow

I would like…
To be a messenger of His love
And share with you
His tranquil and lasting peace
He called me by name
If you listen to your heart
He will do the same

I would like...
Your life to no longer be aimless
He's a faithful compass
A map for our journey
As sturdy as a rock
Yes, my Friend's sweet name
Is none other than Jesus

2013

If They Only Knew

If they only knew
Who I really am
Would they still
Love me
Respect me
Or even care

If they only knew
Who I really am
Would I still
Be here
Doing what I'm doing
Being what I'm being

If they only knew
Who I really am
Sometime saint
And sometime sinner
Yet, I am what I am
And God loves me

2003

In My God I Boast
(Inspired by Psalm 34)

In my God I boast
With His praises on my lips
I will bless the Lord

Let the humble hear
Together let us praise God
Honouring His Name

From all my terrors
I implore God to free me
The Lord answered me

Angels of the Lord
Encamp around me always
Ensuring safety

Come children and hear
Happy those who seek refuge
In the Lord our God

Glorifying God
Together let us praise Him
Now and for ever

Seek and strive for peace
Taste and see the Lord is good
The Lord hears our call

2018

In Praise Of The Trinity

Praise God in heaven above
Thank You for Your love
The great gift of Your Son
Our victory He has won

Praise Jesus our Lord
Such an undeserved reward
Your sacrifice on the Tree
Has set us totally free

Praise the Holy Spirit
Our treasure without merit
Anoint us with Your special gift
To give our earthly life a lift

Glory and honour and praise
Lead us from this earthly haze
May we rely on You the most
Father, Son and Holy Ghost

2002

In This Time Of Lent

(Inspired by the Liturgy of the Hours)

In this time of Lent
With a gift of sacrifice
We praise You O Lord

Instruct us dear Lord
In the ways of Your Kingdom
And bless us always

Please empower us
With a spirit of prayer
And of repentance

Father of mercy
Help us spread justice and love
Throughout the whole world

Make us instruments
Of holy peace and goodness
For all Your people

Forgive us our sins
For failing to see Jesus
In the needy poor

In this time of Lent
May our penance and fasting
Make all things brand new

As we praise You Lord
May resurrection glory
Always cleanse our souls

2019

Into Eternal Life

The seeds of friendship
With our loving God
If watered and cared for
Will bear much fruit
And blossom into eternal life

2019

Jesus

*(Dedicated to the memory of my father Jean-Marie
—based on a traditional Irish text)*

Jesus near and close at hand
Jesus behind and before me stand
Jesus with me wherever I go
Jesus around me, above and below

Jesus in my heart and on my mind
Jesus within my soul be enshrined
Jesus control my wavering heart
Jesus abide in me and never depart

Jesus my life and my only way
Jesus my night lantern and light of day
Jesus my never changing friend
Jesus my guide and shepherd to the end

2019

Jesus Is The Reason

On that most holy first Christmas day
In a shabby wooden stable full of hay
Even though the place was forlorn
A very, very special Child was born

Angels came to sing His praises
They sang the greatest song of the ages
'Glory to God, glory to God in the highest'
And to nearby shepherds they witnessed

In awe and fear they left their sheep
Despite the late hour and fighting sleep
They reached the stable—home of livestock
To witness the biggest miracle of the epoch

In the manger was the Baby the Angels sang about
Next to Mary His mother and Joseph so devout
God out of deep love and mercy became one of us
Jesus, God's Son the most blessed gift of Christmas

May we always cherish Jesus in our heart
Let us pray together and do our just part
To spread the news that Jesus is the reason
For this most blessed and holy Christmas season

2009

Jesus My Shepherd

(Inspired by Psalm 23)

Jesus, You are my Shepherd
You call me to Your chosen herd
To be one of Your sheep
That for ever you will keep

With You there is no peril
And I fear no evil
Following You is key
For You always comfort me

When I observe Your decree
Goodness and mercy follow me
You lead me to pastures green
And on You I can always lean

Your gift of the Tree
Has forever set me free
So, down on my knee
I humbly plea

In Your house may I dwell
As You help me to excel
My life long endeavour
Is to be with You for ever

2002

King Of The Nations
(Inspired by Revelations 15:3-4)

Mighty wonderful
Are Your works God Almighty
King of the Nations

For ever righteous
And true are Your Ways, O Lord
King of the Nations

Who would dare refuse
The great glory due Your Name
King of the Nations

May all worship You
Mighty and clear are Your Deeds
King of the Nations

All people shall come
Since You alone are Holy
King of the Nations

2012

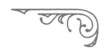

Know Jesus

(Inspired by a circling e-mail)

No Jesus
No cross
No resurrection
No peace

Know Jesus
Know the cross
Know the resurrection
Know Peace

2004

Let Us Share God's Story

With awe let us share God's story
Let us bow before God's throne
To everyone let us proclaim
God's great and magnificent name
Remembering to God alone
We give all praise and glory

At the beginning of creation
In the great heavens up above
Out of the darkness of the shade
In God's image we were made
To show God's unfailing love
God offers us the gift of salvation

So today it is only right
As we continue to journey along
To surrender to God our heart
And to others God's love impart
Let us praise God with song
Witnessing to God's wonder and might

With awe let us share God's story
Let us bow before God's throne
To everyone let us proclaim
God's great and magnificent name
Remembering to God alone
We give all praise and glory

2005

Let Us Sing

(Inspired by Psalm 95)

Today listen to God's voice
The Lord alone is God
God offers us a choice
Mighty is our saving God
We are the apple of God's eye
God's love God will never deny

God molds us in the Lord's hands
God made the waters of the sea
God gives us the dry lands
Let us serve God boldly
Come let us bow down
Shouting God's renown

Come let us sing to the Lord
Approach God with singing
Living in one accord
Singing our thanksgiving
No longer crying dirges
Joyfully shout God's praises

The Lord is our Shepherd
We are the sheep of God's flock
Our prayers God answered
God eyes us like a hawk
God protects us with God's rod
Let us sing praises to our God

2005

'Lift High The Cross'
(Inspired by various spiritual writers)

The great gift of Easter is hope
Christian hope, which gives us confidence
Confidence in God's ultimate triumph
Confidence in God's goodness and love
Which nothing on earth can shake
Let our resurrection joy
Lift us from loneliness
From weakness and despair
To confidence in God
For strength and security
For beauty and happiness

The glorious and joyful news
That Jesus is Risen
Gives new meaning to life
Still before us lie
Work, discipline and sacrifice
Yet, the fact of Easter gives us
The spiritual power and grace
To do the work, accept the discipline
And make the sacrifice

Easter is the Father's demonstration
That life is essentially spiritual
And like God's love timeless
This Easter by God's grace
Let us claim our victory
Over Satan, sin and death
And boldly 'lift high the Cross'

2011

Light Of Heavenly Glory

(Inspired by the Liturgy of the Hours)

Day is dawning ever nearer
Reflecting our Father's love
From the shadow of darkness
Freeing us with Your light

Springing from eternal glory
Jesus, true Son shine upon us
With Your everlasting radiance
Bringing strength to body and soul

Through the Holy Spirit's power
Enkindle in us Your saving fire
Burn away our many failings
With Your sacred cleaning flame

Spread Your rays of splendour
With Your light of heavenly glory
Where Your power is concealed
Giving us hope of life eternal

Glory be to God the Father
Glory be to the Son of Light
Glory be to the enflaming Spirit
Glory now and for all ages

2019

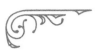

Like A Fish...
(Inspired by St. Jean-Marie Vianney)

Like a fish, which at first swims
on the surface of the water
then afterwards plunges down
and always going deeper

Our soul is also invited to plunge
losing itself in the sweetness
of conversing with our loving God
from heaven down to earth

Like a fish, let us always feed
on the life-giving waters
of God's sanctifying grace
and always dive deeper

2008

Like A Pumpkin

(Inspired by a circulating e-mail)

A Christian is to be like a pumpkin
Chosen to be part of God's royal kin
God picks you out of any old patch
Brings you to God's very special batch
God washes off all the mud and dirt
Like a freshly laundered white shirt

Then God cuts off your top
But that is not where God will stop
The yucky stuff out God scoops
Making you part of God's holy troops
God removes the seeds of doubt
Hate, greed, so you can be devout

God carves you a smiling face
And gives you a very special place
God puts inside of you a blessed light
So you can shine to the entire world bright
Is your light shining and reflecting God's love
This sacred gift from heaven up above

2002

Like A Puzzle
(In thanksgiving for my friends)

Friendship is like a puzzle
Each friend is a unique piece
Some are at the centre
Others are on the border
Still others in the between

Yet each special friend
Is a critical piece
For together we form
The whole picture
That makes us who we are

Life without friends
Is definitely incomplete
So thank you friends
For being important pieces
In the puzzle of my life

2004

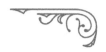

Like A River

(Inspired by a circulating email)

Let us try to live
    like a river
The river never runs
    in the opposite direction

Let us forget our past
    and our failures
Let us live today
    with joy and confidence

Focusing on our future
    and the promise of heaven
Yes, the Lord is preparing us
    a heavenly dwelling

In the opposite direction
    the river never runs
So, let us try to live
    like a river

2019

Like A Teddy Bear

(Inspired by a resident of Covenant House)

Learn to be like a teddy bear
A welcoming and beautiful sight

Learn to listen like a teddy bear
Ears always open and mouth closed tight

Learn to forgive like a teddy bear
With a caring heart, not worried who is right

Learn to love like a teddy bear
Arms wide open and imperfect eyesight

Learn to be like a teddy bear
Warm and without judgement day or night

2019

Like A Sunflower

From the garden in my yard
I see the golden sunflower
It stands tall and on guard
With strength and power

From the many little seeds
Deep in the earth it must die
God gives each one what it needs
To be able to reach the sky

So, it seems to preach to me
As it follows the way of the sun
And gently guides and teaches me
In turn to follow God's Son

May I forever be like a sunflower
And continually focus on the Son
To be strengthened by His power
And the gift of salvation He has won

2019

Like Honey

I believe it was a summer or two ago
I remember that day the sun was aglow
A stranger came calling at my door
I didn't remember seeing him before

It was an out-of-town beekeeper
What he looked like is all a blur
He was selling a fresh batch of honey
Discounted so I could save some money

This discount was for that day only
However, the honey seemed dark and cloudy
He said it was the best honey by far
Cautiously I purchased just one jar

He suggested at this price I buy more
Nevertheless, I told him I had plenty for sure
The salesman graciously wished me well
And thanked me for answering the bell

I sampled the product after he had gone
It had the best flavour I ever came upon
Disappointed with myself I was a little sore
He knew his honey I should have bought more

Similarly, I was hesitant to start reading the Bible
Today by God's grace I know no book is its equal
The more I read the better becomes each foray
Yes, like honey God's words taste sweeter every day

2003

Like The Morning Dew

Just like the morning dew
God's mercy is every day anew
Drenching everything under the sky
It is subtly poured upon you and I

The soaking of grace comes automatically
Yet somewhat unexpectedly
It gently saturates throughout the night
So all is soaked with grace by morning light

As the Lord knocks at our door
Let us receive God's mercy forevermore
Mercy like the morning dew
Only lasts for a short moment or two

As at dawn mercy brings a new day
Leading us in God's sacred way
Let us overcome our daily strife
Claiming God's gift of eternal life

2016

Live Fully Today

(Dedicated to the memory of Darlene O'Hare)

Oh, she was so very young
No one knew her time was done
There was to be many tomorrows
Now we are left only with sorrows

She would not want us to cry
She gave life her very best try
She lived with vim and vinegar
Now God has other plans for her

Her life and death were not in vain
From her a life lesson we should gain
Yesterday is over; tomorrow is the future
So, live fully today and be the victor

Please remember my dear friend
She knew that death was not the end
Let us live fully today, which is still at hand
And prepare for our heavenly homeland

2003

Look Beyond

Look beyond the clouds of life
You'll find the love of heaven
Despite the struggles and daily strife
Count your many blessings given

If we stop and really ponder
Life is not as bad as we think
Yes there might be some clamour
Therefore with God let us be in sync

Take the time to smell the roses
And to enjoy a sunset or sunrise
Consider all the beauty creation bestows
Like colourful rainbows and butterflies

The sound of children's laughter
Or the smile of a newborn baby
Be at peace and your life will alter
So trust in God and no longer be unhappy

2003

Lord Come To My Aid

(Based on Psalm 70)

Lord come to my aid
God make haste to rescue me
Shame my oppressors

Lord come to my aid
Turn them back in confusion
Those who seek my life

Lord come to my aid
Let them retreat shamefully
Who jeer at my lot

Lord come to my aid
Fill me with gladness and joy
With all who seek you

Lord come to my aid
I acknowledge 'God is great'
I cherish Your gifts

Lord come to my aid
My rescuer and helper
Lord do not delay

2019

Lord Have Mercy

(Inspired by the Liturgy of the Hours)

Lord, You went up to Jerusalem
    to suffer and enter into Your glory
Lord bring your earthly Church
    to the heavenly Passover feast
Lord have mercy

Lord, You were lifted high on the Cross
    and pierced by the soldier's lance
Lord always cleanse us
    and heal our wounds
Lord have mercy

Lord, You made the Cross
    the Tree of Life
Lord give its saving fruits
    to those reborn in baptism
Lord have mercy

Lord on the Cross You forgave
    the repentant thief
Lord in Your love and mercy
    forgive us our sins
Lord have mercy

Lord through Your Cross
and sacred Passion
Lord deliver us for ever
From everlasting death
Lord have mercy

Lord You are our Saviour
and Holy Redeemer
Lord save us by Your death
and glorious Resurrection
Lord, have mercy

2019

Lord I Pray

My Lord I come to You in complete humbleness
Help me to recall that I am Your chosen son
I offer You my sinfulness and brokenness
My salvation on the Cross, for me, You have won

Teach me to give as You give and do my just part
Help me to be open to change without delay
Destroy the spirit of selfishness in my heart
Help me to no longer be a Christian *manqué*

Through Your sacramental gifts may I never stray
Lord grant me your peace as I follow You this day
Please lead and guide me to Your heavenly gateway
This I bring before You Jesus: this Lord I pray

Amen

2003

Lord, I Call To You

(Inspired by Psalm 28)

Lord, I call to You
You are my rock and fortress
Hear my pleading voice

I call for Your help
I lift my hands in prayer
To Your holy place

You speak words of peace
You, Lord are my strength and shield
In You my heart trusts

Save us Your people
Bless our heritage today
Carry us always

2018

Lord May...

Lord may every good thing that comes from You
    fill my heart and increase my faith

Lord may Your loving kindness console and
    strengthen me as You promised

Lord may the saving water and blood
    that flowed from Your side on the cross
        cleanse me of my sins and gladden my soul

Lord may the splendour of Your light shine
    rays of hope from heaven to earth

2016

Love In The Hands Of Jesus

People brought infants and little children to Jesus
That He might lay His hands on them and pray
However, the disciples tried to stop them
Jesus said: "Let the little children come to me
Do not stop them for it is to such as these
That the kingdom of heaven belongs
For heaven is open to those who are child-like"
Then He took them in His arms and blessed them
There is always—love in the hands of Jesus

When Jesus came down from the mountain
A leper came to Him and knelt before him
Saying: "If You choose, You can make me clean"
Moved with pity Jesus said: "I do choose to"
He stretched out His hand and touched him
"Be made clean and as Moses commanded
Show yourself to the priest" this Jesus said
Before He withdrew to a deserted place to pray
There is always—love in the hands of Jesus

The scribes and Pharisees brought a woman to Jesus
"This woman was caught committing adultery"
To test Him: "Now what do You say?" they said
"For the law of Moses commanded us to stone her"
"Let the one who is without sin throw the first stone"
Leaving one by one they left her alone with Jesus
"Neither do I condemn you—Go and sin no more"
There is always—love in the hands of Jesus

Jesus on the night that He was betrayed
Took bread in His hands, blessed it and broke it
Saying: "This is my Body, which is given for you
Take this and divide it among yourselves
Do this in remembrance of me"
Then He took a cup of wine and gave thanks
Saying: "This is my Blood of the covenant
Which is poured out for many"
There is always—love in the hands of Jesus

Jesus mounted Calvary hill carrying the wood
There they nailed His hands and feet to the cross
And hung Him on the curse of a tree to die
From the cross Jesus cried: "Father forgive them"
Breathing His last; they placed Him in a tomb
However, on the third day He rose again in glory
And now sits at the right hand of the Father
With trust, let us put our hands in His hands for
There is always—love in the hands of Jesus

2019

Love One Another
(Based on Romans 12:9-16)

Love one another
Hate evil; hold on to good
Love must be sincere

Respect each other
Work and do not be lazy
Faithfully serve God

In struggles patience
Let your hope keep you joyful
And pray at all times

Share all your blessings
Open your home to strangers
And to those in need

Ask God to bless them
Yes those who persecute you
Bless them do not curse

Weep with those who weep
Be happy with the happy
Have concern for all

Do not be too proud
But accept humble duties
Do not claim wisdom

Love must be sincere
Hate evil; hold on to good
Love one another

2003

Love's Trinity

True love has a great affinity
To God in the most Holy Trinity
The Father, Son and Holy Ghost
This union reflects love the most
Mind, heart and soul are requisites of love
Modeled on this blessed union of God above

Love must be a conscious decision of the mind
Not something one enters completely blind
Love always encompasses our entire heart
Never only this or that little part

True love must touch our whole soul
And should really be our life long goal
Trying to love without mind, heart and soul
Leads to nothing but a lifeless hole
Giving rise to hurt and bitter misery
With no future and only a sad history

Love entails this trinity of mind, heart and soul
This sacred and holy triad united as a whole
Yes, love is a blessing of mind, heart and soul
A precious gift from God for all to extol

2002

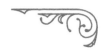

Make My Heart...

Make my heart a Bethlehem
May Jesus be born in me again
Make my heart a Bethlehem
For this I reverently plea

Make my heart a Nazareth
May I live every day as Jesus did
Make my heart a Nazareth
For this I reverently plea

Make my heart a Calvary
May I carry my cross daily
Make my heart a Calvary
For this I reverently plea

Make my heart a Jerusalem
May I experience the gift of heaven
Make my heart a Jerusalem
For this I reverently plea

2019

Mary Leads Us To Jesus
(Inspired by and adapted from Venerable Archbishop Fulton Sheen)

O gracious Father, who made the shining sun
You also made the wondrous moon
The gift of the moon does not take away
From the brilliance of the sun
Without the sun the moon is nothing
All the moon's light is a reflection of the sun

By Your grace, You gave us Mother Mary
A shining heavenly star for us to follow
Our Holy Mother reflects the gift of Her Son
Who is a sacred reflection of Your Divine Light
Without blessed Jesus, Mary is nothing
With Him, She is the blessed Mother of humanity

As the moon leads us to the shining sun
So too, Mary leads us to Jesus, Your sacred Son
Through Mother Mary's guidance and prayers
May we come to love, honour and serve You
In Jesus Christ, Your Son, our Lord and King
Our Holy Redeemer and Saviour of the world

2019

May...

May my trust in you, Lord, not be in vain

May every good thing that comes from you, Lord
    fill my heart and increase my faith

May your loving kindness console and
    strengthen me as you promised

May the saving stream of water and blood that
    flowed from your side, on the cross
        cleanse me of my sins and gladden my soul

May the splendour of your light shine rays of hope
    from the heavens to all the earth

2006

May I Rest In You

(A poetic adaptation of an Edward Hays prayer)

O Beloved, Your song of love
Heard solely by the ears of the heart
Is a silent one from above
Alleviate my fears; Your peace impart

I confidently pray this evening
For my friends and family
With You all will be blessing
Protect those so dear to me

My heart and soul may You keep
Grant me restful dreams tonight
May the sacrament of sleep
Refresh my being with Your light

Creator of the stars beyond counting
I love You Lord with all my might
I humbly come to You for the asking
Untroubled may I rest in You this night

Amen

2003

May The Lord

(Based on the priestly blessing from Numbers 6: 24-26)

May the Lord continually bless you
May the Lord always take care of you
May the Lord favourably look upon you
May the Lord's kindness be showered upon you
May the Lord graciously love you
May the Lord's peace always be with you

Amen

2003

Mommy Please

Mommy, please give me a chance
My life has just begun
I want to learn to sing and dance
To play and have some fun

I know you're scared and young
Yet, Mommy did you even tell Dad
Please, my life has just begun
I am sure Daddy won't be mad

Don't you remember what he said
He always wanted a son or daughter
So, don't let your heart be misled
Think of us before the slaughter

I want to learn to sing and dance
Mommy, please give me a chance

2021

Mother Mary

(A poetic adaptation of the Hail Mary prayer)

Hail Mary full of grace
In our hearts you have a special place
Blessed are you among women
Watch over us your children

The Lord is with thee
So, hear our humble plea
Since the fruit of your womb is blest
Help to save us from this mess

Holy Mary Mother of Jesus the Son
Lead us to the salvation He has won
Pray for us sinners now
To be with You—if God will allow

2002

My Firm Foundation

(Dedicated to my alma mater Cathedral Boys'
High School, Hamilton, Ontario)

As I pass by my old school building
From dreamy sleep old memories are waking
I try to remember the past filled with happy days
But I find myself mostly in a foggy haze

Yet, I recall the school's firm foundation
A necessity for a good solid education
My school was built on the rock of Jesus
Whose strength and guidance are ageless

When my life takes unexpected turns
And my heart and soul are full of yearns
I give God glory, honour and laud
Standing firm and tall I trust in God

With Jesus as my firm foundation
And heaven my eternal destination
There is definitely no mistakin'
On my journey I will not be shaken

2004

My Heart Cries Out

(Inspired by The Confessions of St. Augustine)

My voice is silent
    Yet, my heart cries out
Lord, You know me
    Help me know You

You give my soul strength
    Make it Your dwelling place
Let me know You
    As I am known by You

This is my eternal hope
    The reason I humbly pray
For You have made me
    I am but dust and ashes

O Lord, You are my judge
    You know all of me
You know my hidden self
    I confess my unworthiness

Lead me not into temptation
    Deliver me from evil
Enlighten my darkness
    With the light of Your face

I will be forever restless
    Until I rest in You

2013

My Heart Is Ready

(Based on Psalm 57)

Shine on earth your light
Above the heavens arise
My Lord and my God

I will sing Your praise
My heart is ready, O Lord
My heart is ready

Awake, lyre and harp
Yes, I will awake the dawn
I will thank You Lord

Among the people
Your love reaches the heavens
Your truth to the skies

Shine on earth your light
Above the heavens arise
My Lord and my God

2011

My Pain

I fall on my knees in prayer
I ask God to please forgive her
Why did she not even tell me
Even if we might disagree

I thought she really loved me
Yet, she's too afraid to confide in me
Now it is too late our child is dead
I can't stop crying my eyes are red

My child, this poor innocent life
Has paid the price with a knife
Dear Lord take my pain away
Please answer my plea without delay

Why not adoption, yes adoption
This would have been the loving option

2002

My Religion Is Kindness

*(Adapted and expanded from a poem by Paul Martin for
the 2019 Facer Festival in St. Catharines, Ontario)*

My religion is kindness
said Jesus to me softly
I am here to help you
and keep you company

My religion is kindness
said the morning to the sun
I enable you to rise
when the night is done

My religion is kindness
said the earth to the seed
Trust and I will care for you
I'll fill your every need

My religion is kindness
said the flower to the bee
Come and take my nectar
it's a gift to you from me

My religion is kindness
said the apple to its tree
Help me not to fall
before it's time to pick me

My religion is kindness
said the husband to his wife
Let's share our love with everyone
and we'll have a better life

My religion is kindness
said the mother to her son
We've learned a lot together
and many blessings we have won

My religion is kindness
said the participants at *Facer Festival*
Let's respect one another
making our community better for all

My religion is kindness
said Jesus to me softly
I am here to help you
and keep you company

2019

My Whole Life Long

(Inspired by the Liturgy of the Hours)

From the rising of the sun to its setting
I glorify Your name O Lord for ever
You are the Alpha and the Omega of my faith
Ever on my lips, I bless You with a song of praise

Lord, You called me out of darkness
Into Your marvelous heavenly light
You enabled the blind to see and the deaf to hear
I will bless You Lord my whole life long

I rejoice heartily in You, my Lord
With a mantle of love You wrapped me
My God, You are the joy of my soul
For You have clothed me with the robe of salvation

Yes, my soul gives praise to You, O Lord
I know and fix in my heart that you are God
I will celebrate Your love all my days
Making music to You my whole life long

2018

O Come Bless The Lord

(Based on Psalm 134)

O come bless the Lord
All who stand in the Lord's house
All who serve the Lord

In the house of God
Lift up your hands in prayer
Bless the Lord each night

May the Lord bless you
Who made both heaven and earth
O come bless the Lord

2007

O Holy Sprit

As on that first Pentecost
When all seemed lost
O come Holy Dove
From heaven up above

Show us God's face
And keep us truly safe
Descend upon us
And be among us
Put Your fire in our heart
So we can do our part

Grant us the gift of prophecy
To continue Your legacy
Give us a vision
To overcome division

Let us dream the dream
To accomplish God's regime
Help us make the right decision
To fulfill the Lord's commission
O come great Paraclete
Anoint us to make God's reign complete

2002

O Jesus My Friend

Dear Jesus
You are my friend
You are the Son of God
Come down from heaven

As one of your chosen
In your eyes I am prized
You took me in your arms
I am your precious lamb

With your own hands you offered
A meal of bread and wine
The gift of the Eucharist
Is a life-giving treasure

By sharing your Body
I am nourished and strengthened
I will love you for ever
O Jesus my friend

2019

O Save Me
(Inspired by Psalm 3)

O from harm lift me
O shield me as I cry out
O Lord raise me up

O bless Your people
O Lord of my salvation
O save me my God

2018

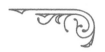

Of God

In the freshness of the dew
Smell the breath of God

In the beauty of creation
See the hand of God

In our longing hearts
Feel the love of God

In the most sacred host
Taste the Son of God

In the quiet of silence
Hear the voice of God

2004

Open The Window To My Heart

Open the window to my heart, Lord
Open the window to my heart
It is torn all apart, Lord
Open the window to my heart

Send me Your healing light, Lord
Send me Your healing light
Shine it brightly on me, Lord
Send me Your healing light

Open the window to my heart, Lord
Open the window to my heart
It is torn all apart, Lord
Open the window to my heart

Cover me with Your saving love, Lord
Cover me with Your saving love
Shadow me with Your love, Lord
Cover me with Your saving love

Open the window to my heart, Lord
Open the window to my heart
It is whole once again, Lord
Open the window to my heart

Thank You for Your gift of peace, Lord
Thank You for Your gift of peace
You give me new life, Lord
Thank You for Your gift of peace

> Open the window to my heart, Lord
> Open the window to my heart
> It is whole once again, Lord
> Open the window to my heart

Open the window to my heart, Lord
Open the window to my heart

2019

Ornament Of Love

A child's soft gentle touch
A precious ornament of love
Though innocent it means so much
Like God's love from above

A child's smiling happy face
A precious ornament of love
Though simple it's full of grace
Like God's coming from above

A child's daily laughter
A precious ornament of love
The great prize our hearts chase after
Like living with God above

A child's dream of up above
A precious ornament of love

2004

Our Glorious Song

(Inspired by Pope St. John Paul II)

We are in God's continual care
Let us not abandon ourselves to despair
We are an Easter People
Let us shout it from the highest steeple
With God we cannot go wrong
And 'Alleluia' is our glorious song

2017

Our True Joy And Hope

As we approach the autumn of our days
We weather the zigzags of life
Benefiting from the journey's recurring seasons
We are grateful to the Creator for our blessings

With the expectant night just around the corner
We learn from the multiple lessons of yesterday
As we realize that eternity is almost upon us
We strive to live faithfully one day at a time

Our riches and earthly possessions fleeting
They are here today and gone tomorrow
We know what 'is' and 'is not' important in life
So, we treasure the gift of the present

Learning from yesterday, we trust in tomorrow
As we serve all our neighbours Samaritan-like
With our true joy and hope for the real future
Being our friendship with the Lord Jesus

2006

Peace

Peace is like a great puzzle

Each of us plays a big part

Are we fulfilling our role?

Come together as a team

Every day and for always

2003

Peace On Earth

(A Christian adaptation of a Chinese proverb)

If you allow the Light of Christ into your soul
There will be a great beauty in your person
If there is a great beauty in your person
There will be a spirit of openness in the family
If there is a spirit of openness in the family
There will be a vital harmony in the home
If there is be a vital harmony in the home
There will be a significant order in the nation
If there is a significant order in the nation
There will be peace on earth our ultimate goal

2002

Please Give Us

(An adapted prayer)

Please give us Your strength Lord
    for sometimes things get tough
And we are ready to quit
    because it is so rough

Please give us Your love Lord
    because sometimes people reject us
And we are tempted to be
    filled with disdain, hate and to cuss

Please give us Your eyes Lord
    because sometimes life seems only black
And we get truly lost
    having difficulty finding our way back

Please give us Your courage Lord
    because we are often under pressure
And it becomes difficult to continue
    to live in good measure

Please give us Yourself Lord
    because our hearts are made for only You
And we will never really rest
    until we truly rest in You

2002

Please Set Me Free

O Lord, please set me free
I want to be near Thee
Surrounded by Thy love
Close to heaven above

O Lord, please set me free
No longer be greedy
Unmoved and self-serving
And forever battling

O Lord, please set me free
Full of Thy honesty
Respect and dignity
Loving others freely

O Lord, please set me free
I want to be near Thee

2004

Praise The Lord, My Soul

(Based on Psalm 103)

Praise the Lord, my soul
All my being, praise God's name
Praise the Lord, my soul

God forgives all sins
Never forgets to be kind
God keeps me alive

Heals my diseases
And blesses me with true love
And constant mercy

God's anger is slow
With steadfast love I am blest
God forgives quickly

God does not punish
As God should and we deserve
In light of our sins

As high as heaven
Is above the planet earth
So great is God's love

My sins forgiven
Are removed as far away
As East is from West

Praise the Lord, my soul
All my being, praise God's name
Praise the Lord, my soul

2003

Queen Of Heaven

(Inspired by a traditional Marian prayer)

O Queen of Heaven
Rejoice, sing Alleluia
Your Son is Risen

Rejoice and be glad
Your Son is truly Risen
Alleluia sing

2019

Rainbow Signature

The harsh violent storm is finally over
Amongst the many clouds the sun is aglow
Highlighted by a multi-coloured rainbow
Sign of the covenant the heavens cover

A promise sealed with God's rainbow signature
The Lord remembers God's vows to the people
Our glory detailed in the Holy Bible
With our God we have a radiant future

2002

Rejoice And Be Glad

Rejoice and be glad all you baptized
For God's gift of freedom
In God's eye we are prized
Chosen members of the kingdom

God has called us each by name
May we all reach a new height
And never be the same
For we are children of the light

As a family united in prayer
May we always do our best
To work and serve together
God the Trinity, most blest

2002

Retreat

What is a retreat?
It's a special time and a sacred treat
When we can stop and listen
Remembering that Jesus died for us yet is risen
Father help us to be still and know that You are God
Jesus continue to guide us with Your Shepherd's rod
Holy Spirit lead us to forgive and forget
And no longer retain and regret

Lord make us instruments of Your peace
May the turmoil and warring within us cease
'As we are' You love us unconditionally
Continue to direct us happily
Knowing that we are never on our own
And that our hearts are Yours alone
Help us to be whole and complete
Now that is the grace of a real retreat

2019

Sacred Artistry

Sacred artistry
Painted by the hand of God
A beautiful gift

Golden reflections
On the calm ocean waters
Of the setting sun

Yes definitely
There is a God in heaven
Maker of all things

I thank and praise You
For all Your countless blessings
Creator most blest

2019

Says The Lord

(Inspired by Jeremiah 29: 11-14)

I know very well the plans I have in mind for you
    Says the Lord
Great plans for your welfare, not for woe or strife
    Says the Lord
Plans to give you a bright future full of hope

Seek Me with your whole heart, with Me you can cope
    Says the Lord
And when you turn to Me, I will change your lot in life
    Says the Lord
So, as you call and pray, I will always listen and be true

2006

Search...

Search for faith…
You will find hope.
Search for hope…
You will find love.
Search for love…
You will find God!

2003

Seasons

Four blessed seasons
Guided by God in heaven
And the sun and moon

First spring then summer
Autumn followed by winter
Right time for all things

From the budding branch
The cardinal's melody
Sounds spring's arrival

Sunshine and rainfall
Bright fresh flowers and green trees
A summer's delight

Under the rainbow
Of autumn's many colours
The peace of God reigns

Ever changing gift
Winter's white frosted blanket
Snowflakes and ice caps

Lord help me to live
Responsibly on this earth
Entrusted to me

2002

Serve The Lord With Gladness

(Inspired by Psalm 100)

Serve the Lord with gladness
You'll find complete happiness
Know that He, the Lord is God
He protects us with His Shepherd's rod

God made us, we belong to Him
Following Him, He'll fill us to the brim
Cry out with joy all the earth
The Lord never forgets our worth

From the beginning, He is faithful
His love is eternal and merciful
Let us live in one accord
For ever giving thanks to the Lord

2005

Source Of Life

(Inspired by Sr. Briege O'Hare)

Source of the Way
Source of the Truth
Source of the Life
Source of the Bread
Source of the Blood

Bless me in my mind
Bless me in my body
Bless me in my soul
Bless me in my coming
Bless me in my going

Source of Faith
Source of Hope
Source of Love
Source of Life
Source of Resurrection

Bless me in my mind
Bless me in my body
Bless me in my soul
Bless me in my coming
Bless me in my going

2019

Source Of Living Water

(Inspired by Fr. Valentine Krul)

Like a never ending water tap is the Spirit's grace
God's unconditional love our sins efface
This source of living water gives us strength
To heal us the Holy Spirit will go to any length

Beyond our sinfulness God's grace will surpass
We in turn can be compared to a water glass
In trying to change us, God does not count the cost
If we place our glass upside down, we are lost

We are free to say 'yes' and forevermore be blest
Or say 'no' and evermore be trapped in our mess
Upside down, no living water may ever enter
Right side up, we are filled to overflowing and for ever

So let us daily prepare our glass and open our heart
To the Spirit's living water and in His Grace impart
May this never-ending water tap of God's love
Secure for us an eternal home in heaven up above

2015

Special Friend

I have a very special Friend
He is faithful until the end
Came down all the way from heaven
Yes, He loves us that's a given

I hear Him daily call my name
If you listen, He'll do the same
Really take the time every day
To let my Friend show you the way

You guessed it: His name is Jesus
A special Friend to all of us

2008

'Sweet Sunshine'

Life is sacred; life is grand
It offers us many jars of 'sweet sunshine'
The jars come in countless shapes and sizes
You can find your 'sweet sunshine' almost anywhere

There are sunny days and the rainbow after the rain
The colours of autumn or the glitter of a fresh snowfall
The poems of Robert Frost, the plays
    of William Shakespeare
Or the words of your favourite novel
The songs of Frank Sinatra or harmonies
    of a barbershop quartet
Or the glorious music of Johann Pachelbel

The smile of a newborn baby or the laughter of children
The love of family and the time spent with friends
The warmth of a gentle handshake or sensual kiss
The aroma of a special home cooked meal
Or the bouquet of an exquisite red wine
The excitement of chocolate
Or the fresh perfume of a luscious red rose
The joy of a little garden or a prized work of art

Whatever you choose I wish you many days, many years
And many jars of 'sweet sunshine'
Yes life is grand: life is sacred

2003

T.G.I.F.

The Father sent Him from above
To share His unconditional love
He was born a child like you and me
T.G.I.F.—Thank God I'm free

All Jesus ever did was good
Yet He was mostly misunderstood
Never considering the cost of the tree
T.G.I.F.— Thank God I'm free

With thankfulness my arms I raise
Giving God all glory and praise
Jesus died on the cross for me
T.G.I.F.— Thank God I'm free

On the third day Jesus arose
Overcoming our deathblow
Destroying the power of the enemy
T.G.I.F.— Thank God I'm free

Accept Jesus as Saviour in your life
He'll overcome all your strife
Doing for you what He did for me
T.G.I.F.— Thank God I'm free

2005

Take The Time

Walk this day in peace
And in the warmth of the Son
Your trouble He will release
Your joy will not be undone

Take the time every day
To be alone with Him
Slow down, stop and pray
He'll fill you to the brim

So, when you are sad or happy
Don't forget to take the time
Your weary spirit He will free
With the promise of heaven sublime

Yes, take the time today
To be with Jesus and pray

2005

Tell My Parents

*(Dedicated to the memory of my parents
Jean-Marie and Thérèse Hétu)*

If red roses grow in heaven
Lord please pick up a dozen
Put them in my parents' room
So, they can savour its perfume

Please let my parents know
That seeing the colours of a rainbow
I always think of them and grin
Remembering them a smilin'

I know they are not forever dead
So, place your hand upon their head
Reminding them that they are kissed
And in my heart forever missed

So, from their special place above
Tell my parents of my endless love

2016

Thanksgiving

For the beauty of the earth
For the sun and moon and stars
We give You thanks, O Lord

For the gift of glorious life
For the gift of family and friends
We give You thanks, O Lord

For smiles, happy times and laughter
For many joys and blessings
We give You thanks, O Lord

For peace and a bountiful harvest
For food, wine and daily bread
We give You thanks, O Lord

For the Eucharist—the Bread of Life
To help us overcome daily strife
We give You thanks, O Lord

For Your Son, Your gift of love
For Your death and resurrection
We give You thanks, O Lord

For the opportunity to give you praise
And be filled with thanksgiving
We give You thanks, O Lord

2002

That I May Be Just

(Inspired by Psalm 119)

Guide me in your path
I delight in your commands
My heart rejoices

Teach me the demands
Of all your loving precepts
Train me in your law

Your words give me life
Please keep my eyes from falsehood
Make me your servant

I long to see you
In your mercy give me life
To you bend my heart

Your decrees are good
Keep the promise you have made
That I may be just

2018

The Bible

The greatest book ever written
Is the Word of God—the Bible
History of the Jewish people and their children
Is in the Word of God—the Bible

Adam and Eve and stories of all great creations
Are in the Word of God—the Bible
Wisdom Books, Prophets, Psalms and Lamentations
Are in the Word of God—the Bible

The quartet of Matthew, Mark, Luke and John
Is in the Word of God—the Bible
How salvation for us Jesus won
Is in the Word of God—the Bible

The letters of the great Apostle Paul
Are in the Word of God—the Bible
The directions to heaven for us all
Are in the Word of God—the Bible

All we need to know and teach our children
Is in the Word of God—the Bible
Yes, the greatest book ever written
Is the Word of God—the Bible

2002

The Blood Of His Love

Blood is thicker than water
But love is thicker than blood
Yes, even despite the slaughter
We are still God's son or daughter
For His love flows like a flood

Out of love God sent His Son
To save us from our death of sin
Yes, heaven for us Jesus has won
No greater sacrifice was done
Is spite of His sad death—we win

From His hands, feet and side
Flowed the blood of His love
This love for us He did not hide
So, His arms Jesus opened wide
To offer us God's love from above

On a wooden cross for us He died
Yet, on the third day Jesus rose
A more eminent love cannot be denied
Yes, new life for us He did provide
A greater gift of love no one knows

2002

The Christmas Miracle

May we forever take to heart
      the message of the angel
And know the intimacy of
      the Christmas miracle
Remembering that hope was born
      that special night
And out of darkness came
      our eternal promised light

Under the great bright shining star
      Jesus, our Saviour, was born
To free us from our many sins
      so we need no longer be forlorn
May our heart and soul always
      be filled with gladness
As we relive the peace, joy and love
      of that first Christmas

2009

The Climb

(A poetic reflection after a retreat on a mountain)

God called me to this peaceful and sacred place
Where everyone is blest and filled with grace
Here I was led through the pain and darkness of night
To the bright promised dawn of God's eternal light

This special mountain experience was worth the climb
At the summit, I met Jesus again for the first time
I started this long hard journey alone and forlorn
Now in the loving arms of Jesus I am reborn

My rebirth comes from an indestructible seed
Through the living and true Word of God, yes indeed
I rediscovered my 'belovedness' through God's eyes
Now I can see the rainbow despite the rainy skies

Yes, God created me a unique piece of art
This new found joy and direction is but a start
I'm leaving the hurt behind to live anew
   with Jesus and grow
So take the time to go up the mountain
   and look out God's window

2006

The Dancer Of Creation

(Inspired by Catherine Cowley)

Our loving God, the dancer of creation
Who made the azure skies and deep blue sea
The God who placed the stars in the heavens
Is the God who cares for you and me

May the weaving of the carpet of our life
With its multi coloured threads and pattern
Reflect the sacred colours of the Creator
Illustrating God's love that we have learned

We cannot always see God's pattern
Even something we have thought was wrong
Is incorporated into something beautiful
Which was the Dancer's plan all along

Only God sees the whole sacred pattern
We must trust that the Lord will shape our mistakes
Into something new, great, and special
So, a heavenly carpet the Dancer of Creation makes

Let our hearts and souls be full of devotion
In gratitude, to our God, the Dancer of Creation

2022

The Gift Of A Seed

The growth of a seed is
      something miraculous
When planted in fertile soil and
      carefully watered
This tiny hard pellet is
      completely transformed

The handiwork of God is seen
      in this mysterious process
Likewise, the seed of God's Word is
      something miraculous
When planted in our hearts and
      carefully nurtured

This treasure from heaven
      completely transforms us
The handiwork of God is seen
      in our fruitful service
Like the blossoming seeds of
      divine creation

God always turns our seeds into
      something beautiful
Let us forever give praise
      and loving thanks
For the handiwork of God as seen
      in the gift of a seed

2009

The Great Promise

The grey bleak stillness of the fading twilight
Silently etched the sorrow of that first Good Friday
Sharing with us the precious blood of His love
On a simple wooden cross for sins Jesus died

The dream-like gathering of the explosive bright sun
Was assimilated by the cottony clouds on the third day
From wretched lifelessness came the great promise
His eternal Easter Victory over sin and death

2009

The Great Seasons Of Life

(Inspired by and dedicated to Martin Saunders)

The season of autumn
And its glorious rainbow of colours
A time of thanksgiving
For a bountiful harvest
Yet, also a time of death
Life returning to renew the earth

The season of winter
A season of silence
Icy-snow covered horizon
Everything lying dormant
A period of deep cleansing
Stillness awaiting new life

The season of spring
The awakening of new life
Melting snow and fresh growth
The return of nature's melody
With birds and their babes
Rejoicing in the grace of new life

The season of summer
When this new life matures
Pastures of endless green
A glorious effervescent garden
Of colourful wildflowers
An awesome festival of the sun

The four faithful seasons
Of our sacred earthly journey
A celebration of humanity
Under the guidance of the Spirit
Daily praising and thanking God
For the great seasons of life

The spiritual season of summer
With our eternal gift of God's Son
Jesus Christ our Lord and Saviour
As we journey closer to Him in hope
We grow in this blessing of new life
For without Jesus we fade and die

The spiritual season of autumn
Like the changing leaves that die
And return back to the ground
We, too, will return to dust
And the cold hard earth
From hence we came

The spiritual season of winter
This season of death
Is not to be feared
When we will be lying dormant
Awaiting the Resurrection
And our last spiritual season

The spiritual season of spring
Our glorious reward of new life
The eternal promise of God
An eternity of hope, joy and peace
The happiness of seeing God—
The Blessed Trinity face to face

Yes, the four faithful seasons
Of our sacred earthly journey
A celebration of humanity
Under the guidance of the Spirit
Daily praising and thanking God
For the great seasons of life

2004

The Greatest Challenge
Of The Ages

(Dedicated to the tireless workers in the Pro-Life movement)

In today's world some may think we're crazy
Yet, we must not forget a baby is still a baby
Despite the many hardships, struggles and strife
The child within the womb is a sacred human life

Let's remind the world, abortion is not the answer
For this over simplified action is simply murder
If we continue this barbaric form of torture
With dead children we are a world with no future

All human life is a sacred gift from heaven above
Our value is that we are the children of God's love
Yes, regardless of our age, sex, creed or race
Created in God's image we all have a special place

Whether 'weak' through age, sickness or disability
The fact that we are children of God gives us dignity
So, we need to develop respect for life at all its stages
And I believe this is the greatest challenge of the ages

2003

The Hands of Jesus

The hands of Jesus
      touched the sick
So that we could know
      God's true compassion

The hands of Jesus
      welcomed the outcast
So that we could see
      God's total acceptance

The hands of Jesus
      caressed the children
So that we could feel
      God's gentle tenderness

The hands of Jesus
      broke some bread
So that we could taste
      God's Body and Blood

The hands of Jesus
      bore two nails
So that we could experience
      God's unconditional love

2019

The Keys Of Your Mercy

My Lord and my God
I do not know how to love you
My heart feels imprisoned
By the iron bars of my sinfulness
Some of my own doing
Some that others have caused

Uncertainty and fear are my jailers
Lord break me free
Use the dynamite of your love
To blow apart these encaging walls
May the keys of your mercy
Unlock my prison door

Let the fire of your unconditional love
Bring my soul out of these prison walls
Help me to step forth from the rubble
To a new life of grace
As a freed and loved child of God
Learning to love you and others more

2016

The Lord's Love

(Based on Psalm 117)

God's always faithful
The Lord's love for us is strong
All nations praise God

2006

The Lost Season Of Advent
(Inspired by Bishop Daniel Miehm)

We have lost the season of Advent
It seems to be more a time for shopping
Filled with stress, misery and discontent
Rather than a time for reflection and stopping

Isaiah the ancient prophet of hope
Reminds us of the coming of the Lord
So with our challenges we can cope
When we live with God in one accord

John the Baptist in the wilderness cried
Repent for the kingdom is near
Our need to confess cannot be denied
With renewed hearts we make His way clear

As Mother Mary surrendered completely
Let us model her humble devotion
And serve her Son Jesus freely
Since her 'yes' was key to our salvation

Let us prepare our hearts and remember
To celebrate Christmas His First Advent
And to His will daily surrender
In joyful anticipation of His Second Advent

We must reclaim the lost season of Advent
Taking time to ponder in our heart
Our need to refocus and repent
So filled with hope and love let us restart

2005

The Pharisee Of Pharisees

It's easy to put down the Pharisees
And their thinly veil hypocrisies
I am with Jesus when he calls them to task
Challenging them to remove their mask

Wait a minute, have I missed the point today
Perhaps I should reflect without delay
The Pharisee is me, and the bottom line
Their thinly veil hypocrisies are mine

Along with the Pharisees, Jesus is calling me
I need to get my beliefs and actions to agree
Lord Jesus cleanse my hard heart
Help me, as of today, to do my part

To put you first in my life
Despite trials, hardships and strife
My salvation, on the cross, you have won
With you, my good works will not be undone

Thank you, Lord Jesus, for setting me free.
Yes, the Pharisee of Pharisees is me

2002

The Price

Jesus paid the price
With His sacrifice
On the sacred Tree
For you and me

Jesus offered His life
Despite the pain and strife
Not counting His loss
He accepted the Cross

At His great cost
We're no longer lost
No longer is life grim
Since we belong to Him

So, what can we do?
But say 'Thank You'
And love one another
As we follow our Brother

2019

The Rainbow Of Christian Virtues

A rainbow reminds us of the promised covenant
Red is for love and devotion to the One true God
Orange is for prudence and our cautious daily behaviour
Yellow is for our golden faith in the Blessed Trinity
Green is for hope and our life filled with confidence
Blue is for temperance and habits of moderation
Indigo is for justice and belief in fairness for all
Violet is for our fortitude and courage to be true
Let us always follow the rainbow of Christian virtues

2006

The Song Of Moses

(Based on Revelation 15: 3-4)

Lord God Almighty
Great and mighty are Your works
And true are Your ways

King of the nations
All glory Your Name is due
For You are worthy

Righteous Lord and King
Who would refuse You honour
Since You are holy

All nations shall come
And worship in Your presence
Mighty are Your deeds

2008

The Tree Of Life

Through our observance of Lent
Help us to understand the meaning
Of why Your Son was sent
His painful death and glorious rising

May we live in one accord
For bearing our sins and strife
The sacred Cross of the Lord
Has become the Tree of Life

At our side You are our defender
From sin You set us free Lord
You are our protector
You raise us up in glory

You crowned Jesus King of kings
May we serve Him faithfully
Protected by your angels' wings
Praising You—Father—continuously

2012

The True Seven Wonders
Of The World

(Inspired by a circulating e-mail)

I am sure that most people would agree
One of the seven wonders is our ability to see
Yes in my search for answers I am most sincere
So a second wonder is our ability to hear

The next wonder for me means so much
A third wonder the sacred gift of touch
A similar and fourth wonder is to feel
A gift for the heart to no longer conceal

A fifth wonder is our ability to taste
With so many treasures we are graced
All these wonders come to us on God's behalf
So let us enjoy a sixth wonder our ability to laugh

A seventh wonder of the world is our ability to love
So praise God for the seven wonders from above
Yes these are the true Seven Wonders of the World
May they be in and around our hearts impearled

2003

The Words Of My Mouth
(Inspired by Psalm 78)

Give heed, O My people, to My teaching
Turn your ear to the Words of My mouth
I will open My mouth in a parable
And reveal hidden lessons of the past

I, the Lord, gave a command to your ancestors
To make me known to your children
That the next generation might know me
Yes, all the children yet to be born

The things you have heard and understood
The wonders your ancestors have told you
These you will not hide from your children
You will tell it to the next generation

Mightily declare all my glories
And the marvelous deeds I have done
I gave witness to your ancestors
With the love I established on earth

May your hearts be truly filled with grace
May you for ever adhere to My covenant
Give heed, O people, to My teaching
Faithful to the Words of My mouth

2019

This Close

My Lord and my God,

I have never felt this close
As when I receive You in the Sacred Host
With Your arms outstretched on the Cross
You never once stopped to count the cost

With my failures and sinfulness I can cope
Because You give me strength and hope
I always feel Your presence and love
You are a gift to me from heaven above

I believe that if I were the only one
Salvation for me You still would have won
So now as I receive You in the Sacred Host
My Jesus I thank You for being this close

2019

This I Pray

For my sake
When I awake
Fill my sight
With Your light
Make me true
To only You

With Your balm
Bring me calm
To me embrace
Your sweet grace

Since You came
With Your flame
Set me free
And guide me

On a wing
May I sing
Lead me home
To shalom
This I pray
Now and every day

2019

Thy Way, Truth And Light

Where art Thou, O Way?
Bridge over troubled waters
Guideth me onward

Thy Truth is secure
Giveth mine heart faith and hope
To always love Thee

Thy Light leadeth me
On Thy only true right path
Ushering me home

2003

To Serve You

(Inspired by Eucharistic Prayer IV)

God, You created us in Your own likeness
And set us over all creation and the whole world
Yes, from complete chaos and total darkness
We are called to serve You—our God and Lord

Again and again, You offered a covenant to us
Even when we disobeyed You, Your friendship lost
Father, You so loved us that You sent us Jesus
Your only Son, He came to save us not counting the cost

To the poor He proclaimed the good news of salvation
To prisoners, freedom and those in sorrow, joy
He freely died on the cross; His perfect love declaration
Rising, life He would restore and death for ever destroy

That we might no longer live for ourselves but for Him
He sent the Holy Spirit from You, loving Father
Guided by the Spirit, may our lives be like a joyful hymn
Praising, worshipping and serving You, You and no other

2006

Today

Take the troubles of yesterday
And throw them away
Lose them where the winds sway
And the children play

Leave them in the past
Today is where your eyes should cast
Why worry about what may
For tomorrow is still far away

Take the time to smell a rose
In its glorious majestic clothes
Listen to the chanting bird
Its melodic symphony is heard

Yes throw your troubles away
Forget the past without delay
Don't worry about what the future may
Put your faith in today

Believe in Jesus our Light
He will bring you great delight
To be truly happy it's a must
So, today in God put your trust

2019

Total Health

Life is a precious gift from above
Remember we are temples of God's love
We must care for our bodily shrines
Following sacred and healthy guidelines

We are called to serve one another
To care and love are the answer
A positive self-image is a healthy start
With God and others we can play our part

So take your problems off the shelf
And truly be good to yourself
Get the assistance that you need
For in God's eyes you are worth it indeed

So care for yourself and others too
This will help us find God's ways anew
A sign and measure of our wealth
Is how we treasure our total health

2003

Touched By An Angel

(Dedicated to my friend Dorice Haché)

Our friendship is a gift
That gives our hearts a lift
It's sent from our Angel up above
To help us know God's love

When it comes to you and me
Our Angel smiles warmly
The knot our Angel tied
Is secure and not about to slide

Yes, we've been touched by an Angel
And for that I am grateful
Thanks for being a true friend
May this blessing never end

2005

Transfiguration In Children
(An adaptation of a poem of an unknown author)

If a child lives with criticism, he learns to condemn
If a child lives with hostility, she learns to fight
If a child lives with ridicule, he learns to be shy
If a child lives with shame, she learns to feel guilty
If a child lives with tolerance, he learns to be patient
If a child lives with encouragement, she learns confidence
If a child lives with praise, he learns to appreciate
If a child lives with fairness, she learns justice
If a child lives with security, he learns to have faith
If a child lives with approval, she learns to like herself
If a child lives with acceptance and friendship
He learns to find love in the world

2018

Trinity Blest

I am in awe of
You, source of glory and love
Father up above

Cannot be outdone
Our salvation You have won
Jesus Christ the Son

You, I inherit
Giver of gifts sans merit
God, Holy Spirit

God, You are my Light
I love You with all my might
Remain in my sight

O heavenly host
Father, Son and Holy Ghost
May I love You most

I make one request
Of You, may I be possessed
Most Trinity blest

2002

True Love

The path to true love
Is like the passage of dawn
It grows from first light
To the full splendour of day
Let us forever cherish
The sunlight of God's true love

2018

Trust In The Lord

(Based on Psalm 27)

The Lord is my Light
True source of my salvation
I will fear no one

I am not afraid
When evil people attack
And try to kill me

They stumble and fall
Even if armies attack
I am not afraid

I will still trust God
I will see the Lord's goodness
In this present life

So, trust in the Lord
Have faith and do not despair
Yes, trust in the Lord

2006

Unconditionally
(Written on a retreat)

Love unconditionally
Love them for their lack of understanding
Just love them
Be a light for them
And guide them to Me
Yes love them

You are special
They are special
You are all special in My Father's eyes
Just love them
Do not judge them
Just love them

Help them know My love
And your love for them
Do not put in any blocks
Just love them
Allow them to love you too
Yes love them—yes love Me

I offer you peace
It is up to you to accept it
My peace I leave you
I leave you peace
I love you
I know you love Me too

Be at peace
Leave the baggage behind
Know that I love you
You are special and unique
Life is a song
So sing it with love unconditionally

2003

We Are One Body

We are one body, the Body of Christ
Jesus died that we might have life
We are one body, the Body of Christ
And we are never really alone

When we eat his Body and drink his Blood
We live in his love and Jesus lives in us
When we answer the cries of the poor and needy
We live in his love and Jesus lives in us

When Jesus calls let us listen to him
The Way, the Truth, and the Life
Yes, Jesus is our Lord and Saviour
The Way, the Truth, and the Life

At the name of Jesus, every knee shall bend
For we are one Body, the Body of Christ
Let us praise and glorify his name till the end
For we are one Body, the Body of Christ

2018

We Give You Thanks

(Inspired by Psalm 75)

We sing psalms to God
As for me, I will rejoice
Rejoice for ever

Now and for always
The wicked shall be broken
The just exalted

We recount Your deeds
We give thanks to You, O Lord
Yes, we give You thanks

2018

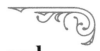

We Give You Thanks O Lord

(Dedicated to St. Margaret Mary Parish, Hamilton, Ontario)

For the glorious azure sky
And the song of birds flying by
We give You thanks O Lord

For rainbow colours of autumn
And seasons' awesome rhythm
We give You thanks O Lord

For the blessing of fertile field
And promises of a bountiful yield
We give You thanks O Lord

For the beauty of the harvest moon
And bright sunlight at noon
We give You thanks O Lord

For the scent of fresh-cut hay
And the twilight at the end of the day
We give You thanks O Lord

For the opportunity to praise You freely
And Your working miracles daily
We give You thanks O Lord

For the Eucharist—the Bread of Life
To help us overcome earthly strife
We give You thanks O Lord

For the gift of family and friends
And Your love that never ends
We give You thanks O Lord

2018

We Really Miss You Emma

(In memory of Emma Ringrose 2000-2005)

Emma, at first, when you died
We were sad and we cried
You were just a young girl
Full of life and a precious pearl

Why did your life have to end?
You were our little friend
We just couldn't understand
'Why?' An answer we demand

But Jesus said: 'Come to Me'
From above the angels saw you happy
So, quickly you were taken up
And now in heaven you worship

We believe that you are not forever dead
To new life you were led
And like the seed that must die
You had to say: 'Goodbye'

Please pray for your friends and family
For we really miss you Emma sweetie
Yet, we know in heaven we'll see you again
And to that we all shout: 'Amen!'

2005

What Friends Are For

Tomorrow is another day
So do not be afraid
I will come to your aid
And help you see His way

That is what friends are for
In good times and bad
So try to smile and be glad
When you see me at your door

Our friend Jesus is really near
Please look into your heart
In your life He wants a part
That my friend is very clear

Let me guide you to a new frontier
To a time and place without fear

2004

What Time Is It?

(Dedicated to the memory of John Dortmans)

If dinner is served at five
Tell me when would you arrive?
If the theatre started at eight
Honestly, would you walk in late?

Arriving at church on time
Now that would truly be sublime
The Mass is a beautiful prayer
Right from the start not only later

In truth, it's not a matter of power
But really I ask: 'What is an hour?'
So, near the end what's the hurry?
Just relax there is no need to scurry

Once a week we're asked to Mass
So, let us celebrate it with class
May I ask again: 'What time is it?'
Time to thank God and pray on it

If dessert is shared at six thirty
Would you still plan to leave early?
If the play ended at about ten
Would you truly leave before then?

2002

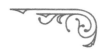

Who Am I?

First camera at twelve
Amateur photographer
Is that who I am?

Actor of the stage
Funny and sad characters
Is that who I am?

He shoots—what a save
Oldtimer golden goalie
Is that who I am?

Priest of God most high
A chosen servant of God
Is that who I am?

Writer in few words
A poetry devotee
Is that who I am?

A blest child of God
Saved by the blood of Jesus
That is who I am!

2002

With Gladness

Daily I have no reason to fear
For You, Jesus my Saviour, are near
Lord, Your love can never be undone
As we walk hand-in-hand as one
To enlighten and guide me each hour
I follow You and trust in Your power

From the dawn of morning light
To the darkness of dusk at night
I serve You Lord joyfully all day
With gladness I follow Your way
Hold me in the palm of Your hand
And lead me to our heavenly homeland

2005

With Joy I Sing Your Praise

O Jesus Christ the Son
Lord, for You, I long
My victory You have won
With You I'm truly strong

With joy I sing Your praise
All laud and honour are due
My arms in prayer I raise
All glory and power to You

Lord lead me to Your peace
As I glorify You each day
With words that never cease
May I always continue to pray

Yes, I worship You in song
To you my spirit I commend
With You alone I belong
Amen! Alleluia! Amen!

2002

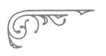

With You Jesus

Jesus, You are my Lord
May You always be near
Guide me into Your sphere
To live in one accord

May Your carpenter's lathe
Lovingly shape my heart
And forever impart
Your Father's gift of faith

My sins You have destroyed
So I will give You praise
Today and all my days
For I am overjoyed

Forever send Your love
Gift from the Spirit's flame
This blessing may I claim
From heaven up above

May You be my true Friend
Holding my open hand
With You Jesus, I stand
United 'til the end

2004

Worthy Of Our Praise

(Based on Revelation 15: 3-4)

Lord God Almighty
Your works are all wonderful
And truly mighty

Who would dare refuse
The glory due Your Name, Lord
And not honour You

All nations shall come
Since You alone are holy
Worthy of our praise

In Your great presence
All Your mighty deeds are seen
Now and for ever

2011

Yes Jesus Loves Me

(Written on retreat)

Love is the answer
Jesus is the answer for us all
Take the time to listen and hear
Yes take the time to listen and hear
Love is the answer
Jesus is the answer

Love is life
Life is love
So take time to love
It is worth it
You are worth it
Yes take time—make time

So where to begin?
Begin with yourself
Yourself and the Lord
Begin with Jesus
There is no right or wrong way
Just begin

You can find Jesus anywhere
Jesus is everywhere
Jesus is where you are
So take time to be with Jesus
Who am I before Him?
A brother, a friend, a journeyer

So take time to be with Jesus
He loves me
Yes He loves me
He wants me to be free
Life is a mystery between two lovers
Jesus and me

He is there for me to discover
Listen to the silence
You will hear Him calling
He calls me by name
Because He loves me
It is simple Jesus loves me

What does this mean?
He wants me to befriend Him
And love Him
Yes Jesus loves me
And wants me to befriend Him
And love Him

Jesus I love You
I want to thank You
For Your gift of life
For Your love and forgiveness
Yes Jesus You know
That I love You

Help me to let go
To let go of doubts
The question about others
To let You love me
As you created me
Yes Jesus I love You

Help to love others
Be with them in the moment
Be present for them and love them
Love them for who they are
Not who I would like them to be
Or who they would like me to be

2003

You Are A Beautiful Person

(Based on a circulating e-mail)

You are a beautiful person

Think if God had a fridge
Your picture on it would be a bridge
Between the glories of heaven and earth
To show all creation your worth

If God had a wallet or purse
Your photo in it would be a topic to converse
God sends you flowers every spring
And you, God is always remembering

A sunrise with every new day dawning
For you to enjoy in the morning
When you're on a nature walk
And you decide that you really want to talk

Creation, for you, God continues to glisten
For God undoubtedly really does listen
Of anywhere, God chose to live in your heart
And know that this is but the start

God did not promise you a rose garden
But your sins God did promise to pardon
Face it God is crazy about you my friend
Know that God's love for you will never end

Please remember, you are a beautiful person

2002

You Are A Gift

(Inspired by the Book of Wisdom)

I loved and sought after you from my youth
 I sought to take you to be my lover
  I was enamoured from the day we met
   For nothing in life is more precious to me

So I was determined to take you with me
 Knowing that you would be my confidant
  While all was well
   And my comfort in time of grief

For loving you involves no bitterness
 And being with you no sorrow
  But rather joy and gladness
   And I marvel at you a blessing

Thinking thus within myself
 And reflecting in my heart
  I could not otherwise love you
   Except by God's graceful gift

So I went to the Lord and gave God glory
 With prudence I treasure you
  Knowing that you are a gift
   And I love you dearly

2017

About The Author

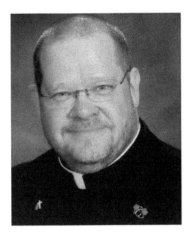

R.J. Hétu, better known to many as Père Robert or Father Robert, is pastor of the four Catholic French language parishes in the Niagara Region in Ontario (Welland, St. Catharines, Port Colborne, and Niagara Falls). R.J. was born and raised in Hamilton, Ontario. He is the second son and fifth child of nine of the late Jean-Marie and the late Thérèse Hétu. On May 10th, 1986, he was ordained a priest for the Diocese of Hamilton in Canada. Fr. Robert was recently elected Dean of Welland.

In 1975, R.J. graduated from Cathedral Boys' High School, Hamilton; in 1979 with a B.A. from St. Jerome's University—University of Waterloo; in 1984 with a M.Div. (Master of Divinity) from St. Peter's Seminary—King's University College—University of Western Ontario, London, Ontario; and, in 2001 with a STM (Maters of Sacred Theology—Magna Cum Laude) from Regis College—Toronto School of Theology—University of Toronto.

He wrote his first poem on retreat in 1998 and second for a radio contest in early 2000. Since winning free concert tickets, he has not stopped writing poetry. Today, he mostly writes faith-based poetry.

Fr. Robert was a high school chaplain at École secondaire catholique Père-René-de-Galinée, in Cambridge, Ontario, for three years. He also served as an elected Catholic School Board trustee for over 17 years. Fr. Robert has been a member of the Knights of Columbus for forty plus years. He has, also, served as Chaplain to various councils over the years. He is currently Chaplain of Conseil Père Edmond #7741. He is also a long-time Fourth Degree member.

R.J. also enjoys dabbling in photography (a hobby since he was twelve), acting in community theatre, tending goal in oldtimers' hockey, and playing tennis. After bilateral knee replacement, he has recently taken up pickleball. He hopes, one day soon, to learn to read music and to play the piano.

Lightning Source UK Ltd.
Milton Keynes UK
UKHW010631150422
401616UK00001B/74